The European Union

Political, Social, and Economic Cooperation

THE
EUROPEAN UNION
POLITICAL, SOCIAL, AND ECONOMIC COOPERATION

The European Union
Political, Social, and Economic Cooperation

THE NETHERLANDS

by
Heather Docalavich

Mason Crest Publishers
Philadelphia

Mason Crest Publishers Inc.
370 Reed Road, Broomall, Pennsylvania 19008
(866) MCP-BOOK (toll free)
www.masoncrest.com

First printing
1 2 3 4 5 6 7 8 9 10

Library of Congress Cataloging-in-Publication Data

Docalavich, Heather.
  The Netherlands / by Heather Docalavich.
      p. cm.—(The European Union : political, social, and economic cooperation)
  Includes index.
    ISBN 1-4222-0057-4
    ISBN 1-4222-0038-8 (series)
  1. Netherlands—History—Juvenile literature. 2. Netherlands—Description and travel—Juvenile literature. 3. Netherlands—Social life and customs—Juvenile literature. 4. European Union—Netherlands—Juvenile literature. I. Title. II. European Union (Series) (Philadelphia, Pa.)
  DJ18.D63 2006
  949.2—dc22
                          2005020101

Produced by Harding House Publishing Service, Inc.
www.hardinghousepages.com
Interior design by Benjamin Stewart.
Cover design by MK Bassett-Harvey.
Printed in the Hashemite Kingdom of Jordan.

CONTENTS

THE NETHERLANDS

European Union Member since 1952

West Frisian Islands

● Groningen

● Leeuwarden

● Sneek

Den Helder ●

● Meppel

Haarlem ●

Almelo ●

⭐
Amsterdam

● Apeldoorn

Enschede ●

● Utrecht

The Hague ●
● Delft

● Arnhem

● Rotterdam

Nijmegen ●

Breda ●

● Tilburg

● Eindhoven

INTRODUCTION

ISixty years ago, Europe lay scarred from the battles of the Second World War. During the next several years, a plan began to take shape that would unite the countries of the European continent so that future wars would be inconceivable. On May 9, 1950, French Foreign Minister Robert Schuman issued a declaration calling on France, Germany, and other European countries to pool together their coal and steel production as "the first concrete foundation of a European federation." "Europe Day" is celebrated each year on May 9 to commemorate the beginning of the European Union (EU).

The EU consists of twenty-five countries, spanning the continent from Ireland in the west to the border of Russia in the east. Eight of the ten most recently admitted EU member states are former communist regimes that were behind the Iron Curtain for most of the latter half of the twentieth century.

Any European country with a democratic government, a functioning market economy, respect for fundamental rights, and a government capable of implementing EU laws and policies may apply for membership. Bulgaria and Romania are set to join the EU in 2007. Croatia and Turkey have also embarked on the road to EU membership.

While the EU began as an idea to ensure peace in Europe through interconnected economies, it has evolved into so much more today:

- Citizens can travel freely throughout most of the EU without carrying a passport and without stopping for border checks.

- EU citizens can live, work, study, and retire in another EU country if they wish.

- The euro, the single currency accepted throughout twelve of the EU countries (with more to come), is one of the EU's most tangible achievements, facilitating commerce and making possible a single financial market that benefits both individuals and businesses.

- The EU ensures cooperation in the fight against cross-border crime and terrorism.

- The EU is spearheading world efforts to preserve the environment.

- As the world's largest trading bloc, the EU uses its influence to promote fair rules for world trade, ensuring that globalization also benefits the poorest countries.

- The EU is already the world's largest donor of humanitarian aid and development assistance, providing 55 percent of global official development assistance to developing countries in 2004.

The EU is neither a nation intended to replace existing nations, nor an international organization. The EU is unique—its member countries have established common institutions to which they delegate some of their sovereignty so that decisions on matters of joint interest can be made democratically at the European level.

Europe is a continent with many different traditions and languages, but with shared values such as democracy, freedom, and social justice, cherished values well known to North Americans. Indeed, the EU motto is "United in Diversity."

Enjoy your reading. Take advantage of this chance to learn more about Europe and the EU!

Ambassador John Bruton,
Head of Delegation of the European Commission, Washington, D.C.

Modern-day windmills across the Netherlands' flat land

CHAPTER 1 THE LANDSCAPE

The Netherlands, like its name suggests, is a low-lying country. About half of the country's territory lies no more than three feet (1 meter) above sea level, and one-fourth of the country is below sea level. **Dikes**, canals, dams, **sluices**, and windmills are distinctive features of the Dutch landscape. They are a critical part of the extensive water drainage system that has enabled the Dutch to expand their country's land area by almost one-fifth. More important, without this constant drainage and the protection of dunes along the nation's coast, almost half of the Netherlands would be flooded—mainly by the

east to west the Netherlands extends 120 miles (193 kilometers), and from north to south the greatest distance is 190 miles (306 kilometers). The Netherlands is bounded on the east by Germany, on the south by Belgium, and on the north and west by the North Sea. The coastline of the North Sea consists mostly of sand dunes. Many of the country's major cities are located on these slightly elevated dunes. In the north, the sea has broken through the dunes to form the West Frisian Islands.

QUICK FACTS: THE GEOGRAPHY OF THE NETHERLANDS

Location: Western Europe, bordering the North Sea, between Belgium and Germany

Area: slightly less than twice the size of New Jersey

total: 16,033 square miles (41,526 sq. km.)

land: 13,082 square miles (33,883 sq. km.)

water: 2,951 miles (7,643 sq. km.)

Borders: Belgium 280 miles (450 km.), Germany 358 miles (577 km.)

Climate: temperate; marine; cool summers and mild winters

Terrain: Mostly coastal lowland and reclaimed land (polders); some hills in the southeast

Elevation extremes:

lowest point: Zuidplaspolder— –23 feet (–7 meters)

highest point: Vaalserberg—1,056 feet (322 meters)

Natural hazards: flooding

Source: www.cia.gov, 2005.

DIKES, DAMS, AND POLDER LAND

In the south, rivers have broken through the dunes and created a ***delta*** of islands and water-ways. Near the narrow strip of dunes is a low-lying area protected by dikes and kept dry by

sea, but also by the many rivers that cross it. Canals, rivers, and coastal inlets cut through much of the low-lying western part of the country. Farther to the east, the land lies slightly higher and is flat or gently rolling.

The elevation rarely exceeds 160 feet (50 meters). Most of the land is devoted to agriculture. The total area of the Netherlands is slightly larger than the states of Massachusetts, Connecticut, and Rhode Island combined. At its widest point from

continuous mechanical pumping. This is *polder land* that the Dutch have reclaimed from the sea and turned into productive farmland. Dikes were built around sections of this swampy or flooded land, and the water was pumped out, at first by windmills and later by steam and electric pumps. Reinforcing dikes were also built along the lower sections of the Netherlands' major rivers, which flow above the land between banks of sediment deposited when they flood.

The lowlying waters and traditional windmills of the Netherlands

The Dutch began efforts to reclaim the Zuider Zee, a large segment of land covered by the North Sea, in 1927. By 1932, a large dike had been built across the entrance to the Zuider Zee. The dike turned the water behind it into a freshwater lake within five years. By the early 1980s, about three-quarters of the area had been drained, but the project to reclaim the last polder was canceled by the early 1980s. The freshwater lake left behind is called the IJsselmeer. In 1953, a spring tide severely flooded the delta region in the southwest, and almost two thousand people died. The Delta Plan, launched in 1958 and completed in 1986, was implemented to prevent such flooding.

Under the plan, the Dutch shortened their coastline by about 435 miles (about 700 kilometers) and developed a system of dikes. They also built dams, bridges, locks, and a major canal. The dikes created freshwater lakes and joined some islands. The polders are used almost exclusively for agriculture and are comprised chiefly of clay soils and peat. Most of the eastern half of the Netherlands is covered by sandy soil deposited by glaciers, wind, and rivers. The nation's only hills are the foothills of the Ardennes. These hills with their fertile loamy soil are found only in the southern part of Limburg Province, an area of rich farmland. Vaalserberg, the nation's highest point, is in this area.

Sixty percent of the nation's population currently lives at or below sea level, making the Netherlands particularly vulnerable to any rise in sea level induced by the *greenhouse effect*. As a result, the Dutch have been at the forefront of calls to reduce dependency on fossil fuels and to bring *deforestation* to a halt. The Netherlands contributes less than 1 percent of global green-

The Netherlands is famous for its tulips.

house emissions. Dutch agriculture depends heavily on the use of fertilizer, and significant nitrate pollution has occurred in water. In addition, pigs and other livestock produce huge amounts of manure and ammonium gas, polluting groundwater resources and affecting vegetation. The government has implemented new policies that require farmers to process manure in ways that are environmentally sound.

RIVERS AND LAKES

The major rivers of the Netherlands are the Rhine, flowing from Germany, and its several **tributaries**, like the Waal and Nederrijn rivers. Other important waterways include the Maas and the Schelde, which originate in Belgium. These rivers and their smaller branches form the delta with its many islands. Together with numerous canals, the rivers give critical shipping access to the interior of Europe.

In the northern and western portions of the Netherlands are many small lakes. Nearly all the larger natural lakes have been pumped dry. However, projects to reclaim land near the coast have created a number of new freshwater lakes, the largest being the IJsselmeer.

A TEMPERATE CLIMATE

The Netherlands enjoys the **temperate maritime** climate that is found across much of Northern and Western Europe. Winds from the North Sea give the Netherlands mild winters and cool summers. Cloudless skies are uncommon, as is prolonged frost. Because the Netherlands has few natural barriers to weather, such as high mountains, the climate varies little from region to region.

The average temperature range in the coastal region is 34° to 41°F (1° to 5°C) in January, and 57° to 69°F (14° to 21°C) in July. In the densely populated central region of the country, the average range is 31° to 40°F (–1° to 4°C) in January and 55° to 72°F (13° to 22°C) in July. Annual precipitation ranges from twenty-seven inches (690 millimeters) to thirty inches (770 millimeters).

TREES, PLANTS, AND WILDLIFE

Over the centuries, human activity has permanently altered the natural landscape of the Netherlands in many ways. Because land is scarce and fully developed, areas of natural plant life are rare. A number of national parks and nature reserves have been established to protect the remaining areas of the natural landscape.

The forests, the tall grasses of the dunes, and the heather of the heaths provide important habitats for roe deer, rabbits, hares, and small numbers of wild boar. The forests, mainly of oak, beech, ash, and pine, are carefully planned and protected by the government. Agricultural land, pastures for grazing animals in particular, provide habitats for many species of migratory birds. Recent environmental projects have increased the number of wetlands, providing habitats for a number of species, including the newly reintroduced beaver and otter.

The Netherlands has a long and rich history.

2 THE NETHERLANDS' HISTORY AND GOVERNMENT

The Netherlands has not always existed as the unified country it is today. For centuries, the area was more of a cultural region than a nation. It was comprised of many territories, each fairly independent and loosely united as a republic. The people of these territories were had a common language, religion, and culture, but they were not united under one centralized government until the establishment

The Netherlands in Ancient Times

The Netherlands has been inhabited since the last **ice age**; the oldest artifacts that have been found are 100,000 years old. During this time, the Netherlands was comprised largely of **tundra** with very scarce vegetation. The area's first inhabitants were **hunter-gatherers** who lived during the last ice age. After the end of the ice ages, various **Paleolithic** groups inhabited

and the Batavii, who had settled there around 600 BCE. The Batavii were sometimes regarded as the "true" forefathers of the Dutch by later **nationalist** scholars.

In the first century CE, the Romans conquered the southern part of the Netherlands, where they built the first cities and created the Roman province of Germania Inferior. For most of the area of Roman occupation in the Netherlands, the boundary of the Roman Empire lay along the Rhine River. Romans built the first cities in the Netherlands. The most important of these were Utrecht, Nijmegen, and Maastricht. The Romans also introduced writing. Even the northern part of the Netherlands that lay outside Roman control was heavily influenced by the civilization that flourished to the south. Roman civilization in the area was eventually overrun by the mass migration of Germanic peoples, later known as the Völkerwanderung.

Dating Systems and Their Meaning

You might be accustomed to seeing dates expressed with the abbreviations BC or AD, as in the year 1000 BC or the year AD 1900. For centuries, this dating system has been the most common in the Western world. However, since BC and AD are based on Christianity (BC stands for Before Christ and AD stands for *anno Domini*, Latin for "in the year of our Lord"), many people now prefer to use abbreviations that people from all religions can be comfortable using. The abbreviations BCE (meaning Before Common Era) and CE (meaning Common Era) mark time in the same way (for example, 1000 BC is the same year as 1000 BCE, and AD 1900 is the same year as 1900 CE), but BCE and CE do not have the same religious overtones as BC and AD.

the area. Later, the first notable remains of Dutch prehistory were erected, the dolmens, which are large stone burial markers. Found in the province of Drenthe, they were probably built between 4100 and 3200 BCE. By the time the ancient Romans arrived in the region, the Netherlands was inhabited by various Germanic tribes, such as the Tubanti, the Canninefates, the Frisians,

After the collapse of Roman authority, the Franks, a Germanic tribe, emerged as the dominant power in the region. Charlemagne, a Frank and the greatest ruler of the era, built an empire that extended over the territory of the Netherlands, Germany, France, and much of central Italy. **Civil wars** followed Charlemagne's death, and his sons divided their father's empire into three kingdoms.

The history of the Netherlands told in stained glass

THE HOLY ROMAN EMPIRE

Eventually, the Frank dynasty died out in Germany and gave way to the Saxons. Otto I, a strong Saxon emperor, founded the Holy Roman Empire in 962 CE. The Holy Roman Empire was a group of Western and Central European territories that stood united by their faith in Roman Catholicism.

While there was one supreme emperor, each territory had its own individual ruler. Constant struggles between these rulers and the empire marked the period. The crown and the Roman Catholic Church were also locked in a power struggle.

At its peak, the empire contained most of the territory that makes up the Netherlands today, as well as modern-day Germany, Austria, Slovenia,

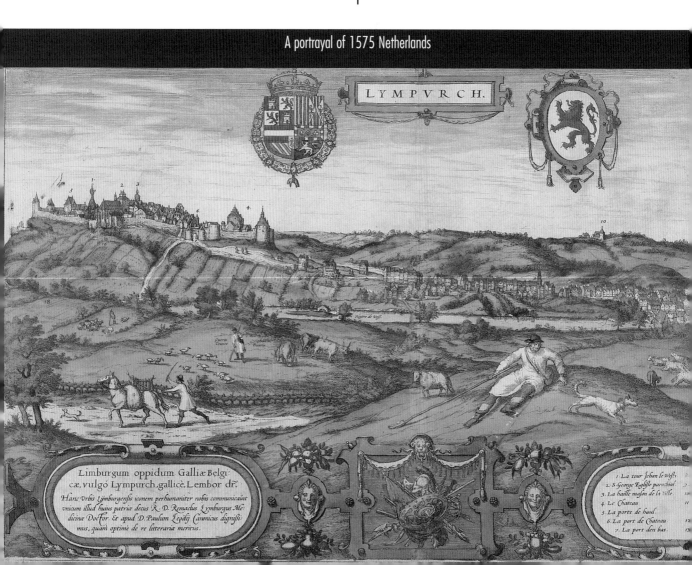

A portrayal of 1575 Netherlands

LYMPVRCH.

Limburgum oppidum Galliæ Belgi-
cæ, vulgó Lympurch, gallicè, Lembor dr.
Hanc Vrbis Lymburgensis iconem perhumaniter nobis communicauit
vnicum illud huius patriæ decus R. D. Remaclus Lymburgus Me-
dicinæ Docfor. & apud D. Paulum Leodij Canonicus dignissi-
mus, quam optimè de re literaria meritus.

1. La tour Ieban le Wost.
2. S. George Eglise parochial.
3. La baille mason de la ville.
4. Le Chateau.
5. La porte de haul.
6. La port de Chateau.
7. La port den bas.

Switzerland, Belgium, Luxembourg, the Czech Republic, eastern France, northern Italy, and western Poland. Unfortunately, The Holy Roman Empire was not able to maintain political unity. The local nobility turned their tiny **principalities** and **duchies** into private kingdoms. There was little sense of obligation to the emperor who governed over many parts of the nation in name only.

The various **feudal** states faced almost continual war, especially Utrecht and Holland. Through inheritance and conquest, the Netherlands eventually became a possession of the Hapsburg dynasty under Charles V in the sixteenth century, who united the different principalities into one state. In 1548, Emperor Charles V granted the Netherlands status as an entity separate from both the Holy Roman Empire and from France. This act, the Pragmatic Sanction of 1548, did not grant the Netherlands full independence, but it allowed significant **autonomy**.

The Reformation and the Eighty Years' War

The sixteenth century brought a new age to Europe: the Reformation. People began to question the practices of the Roman Catholic Church. This led to the creation of a new Christian group, the Protestants, or those who protest. In 1517, Martin Luther, a German monk, led a revolt against the Catholic Church, and Protestant teachings quickly gained a following throughout the region.

Charles V was succeeded by his son, Philip II of Spain. Unlike his father, who had been raised in Belgium, Philip had little interest in the Netherlands and the surrounding areas (otherwise known as the Low Countries) and thus was perceived as cold and detached by the local nobility. A devout Catholic, Philip was disgusted by the success of the Reformation in the Low Countries, which had led to the increasing popularity of **Calvinism** in the region. His attempts to enforce religious persecution of the Protestants and his efforts to centralize government, the justice system, and taxes made him unpopular and led to a revolt.

The Dutch fought for their independence from Spain, leading to the Eighty Years' War (1568–1648). Seven rebellious provinces united in the Union of Utrecht in 1579 and formed the Republic of the Seven United Netherlands. William of Orange, the nobleman from whom every Dutch monarch is descended, led the Dutch during the first part of the war. The earliest years of the war were a success for the Spanish forces. They recaptured Antwerp and other important cities. However, subsequent sieges in Holland were countered by the Dutch, and later developments in the war favored the new republic. It recaptured most of the territory in the Netherlands. The Peace of Westphalia, signed January 30, 1648, confirmed the independence of the United Provinces from Spain.

THE GOLDEN AGE

During the Eighty Years' War, the Dutch began to engage in overseas trade on a large scale. They hunted whales near Svalbard, and traded spices with India and Indonesia via the Dutch East India

IS IT NETHERLANDS OR HOLLAND? AND WHERE DOES DUTCH COME FROM?

Many English-speakers consider Holland and Netherlands to be synonyms, different words for the same nation. Actually, however, Holland used to be a country, but it is no longer. Today Holland is a region in the modern nation of the Netherlands; the old kingdom of Holland is now divided into two provinces, North Holland and South Holland.

The word "Dutch," meanwhile, is used to refer to the language and the people of the Netherlands. It is derived from theodisk, a word meaning "of the people." Some people from the Netherlands prefer the term Netherlandic, since the word Dietsch (the Dutch word for "Dutch") is so similar to Deutsch (the German word for "German").

Company. The Dutch East India Company was the first company in history to issue shares of stock and was responsible for Dutch colonialism. During this period the Dutch founded colonies in Brazil, New Amsterdam (now New York), South Africa, and the West Indies. The Calvinist nation flourished culturally and economically as the dramatic increase in wealth and prosperity began to feed a resurgence in the arts and literature. Due to these developments, the seventeenth century is often called the Golden Age of the Netherlands.

The Netherlands was now a republic, largely governed by an **aristocracy** of city-merchants called the regents, rather than by a king. Every city and province had its own government and laws, and a large degree of autonomy. After attempts to find a competent sovereign proved unsuccessful, it was decided that **sovereignty** would be **vested** in the various provincial estates, the governing bodies of the provinces. The Estates-General, a legislative body with representatives from all the provinces, would decide matters important to the republic as a whole. However, at the head of each province was a stadtholder, a position held by a descendant of the House of Orange. Usually one stadtholder had authority over several provinces.

Following international recognition of the independence of the Netherlands, the republic began to experience a decline. In 1650, the stadtholder William II, Prince of Orange died, leaving the nation without a powerful ruler. Since the conception of the republic, there had been an ongoing struggle for power

DORDRACVM vulgo Dort.
Me Mosa, & Walis, cum Linga, Meruaqué, cingunt,
Æternam Bataue virginis, ecce, fidem.

Sixteenth-century Netherlands

between the regents and the House of Orange. Foreign enemies sought to take advantage of the lack of a strong centralized government in hope of gaining Dutch colonial holdings. A series of wars with England, France, and Spain drained the economy, and by the end of the eighteenth century, political unrest had come to a head.

The Napoleonic Era and the Establishment of the Monarchy

As time went on, there was increasing conflict between the Orangists, who wanted stadtholder William V of Orange to hold more power, and the Patriots, who under the influence of the American and French revolutions wanted a more democratic form of government. In 1785, there was an armed rebellion by the Patriots.

The Orangist reaction was severe. No one dared appear in public without an orange **cockade** for fear of being **lynched**, and a small unpaid Prussian army was invited to occupy the Netherlands by the Orangists. The unpaid soldiers wasted little time before they began supporting themselves with looting and **extortion**.

When the French general Napoleon Bonaparte invaded and occupied the Netherlands in 1795, his troops encountered very little united resistance. William V of Orange fled to England in advance of the French army. The French occupation of the Netherlands ended in 1813 after Napoleon was defeated, a defeat in which William V played a prominent role.

After the Napoleonic occupation, the Netherlands was put back on the map of Europe. In 1815, the country became a monarchy, with William V, the Prince of Orange crowned King William I. By 1848, political unrest across Europe convinced King William II to agree to **liberal** and **democratic** reforms, rewriting the constitution, and transforming the Netherlands into a **constitutional monarchy**. The new document was proclaimed valid on November 3 of that year. As the nineteenth century came to a close, the nation prospered, expanding its colonial holdings in the Pacific, and extending to its citizens freedoms and civil liberties that were very liberal for the age.

The Netherlands and the World Wars

World War I began on June 28, 1914, when Gavrilo Princip, a Serbian nationalist, assassinated Austrian archduke Ferdinand and his wife, Sophie. Russia allied with Serbia. Germany sided with Austria and soon declared war on Russia. After France declared its support for Russia, Germany attacked France. German troops then invaded Belgium, a **neutral** country, as it stood between German forces and Paris. Great Britain declared war on Germany.

Although the Netherlands remained neutral in the conflict, it did not escape unharmed; it was literally surrounded by nations at war. The German invasion of Belgium led to an influx of nearly one million refugees from that country. The North Sea became unsafe for civilian ships to sail, and food became scarce. An error in food distribution caused the aptly named Potato Rebellion in Amsterdam in 1917, when rioters robbed a food transport intended for soldiers.

The Netherlands found itself economically crippled following the war, and the nation's fortunes did not improve greatly as it struggled with the challenges caused by the **Great Depression**.

The Depression led to mass unemployment and poverty, as well as increasing social instability. Riots broke out in Amsterdam, requiring the intervention of the army. Concern was also mounting over the rise of Adolph Hitler in neighboring Germany.

At the outbreak of World War II in 1939, the Netherlands declared its neutrality again. However, on May 10, 1940, Germany launched an attack on the Netherlands and Belgium, quickly overrunning most of the country and fighting against a poorly equipped Dutch army. The nation's rapid defeat, though, affected only the Royal Netherlands Army. The Royal Netherlands Navy, the Royal Air Force, and the Netherlands East Indies Army, stationed in the Dutch East Indies, were still left operational, so the Netherlands did not cease to fight. This proved to be vitally important to the governing of the overseas territories and the continuing resistance against Germany.

The royal family and some military forces managed to escape to Britain before Japanese troops invaded the Dutch East Indies on January 11, 1942. The Dutch, weakened by the Nazi occupation at home, surrendered on March 8, after Japanese troops landed on the island of Java. Dutch citizens were captured and put to work in forced labor camps. However, many Dutch ships and military personnel managed to escape to Australia, from where they were able to continue to fight against the Japanese.

Shortly after the invasion the persecution of Jews began. The Germans established a "Jewish Board" as a way of organizing the identification and **deportation** of Jews more efficiently. When the Germans had gathered enough information, they started deporting the Jews to **concentration camps**. The Dutch people protested the deportations with a strike, which accomplished little except to encourage the Germans to impose harsher restrictions on the occupied Dutch. The consequences for the Jewish community were catastrophic; less than one-quarter of all Dutch Jews survived the war. Perhaps the nation's best recognized victim of the Holocaust is Anne Frank, a young girl who became famous years later because of her diary, written while she was in hiding from the Nazis. The Franks were eventually found, and Anne died in a concentration camp.

The occupied Dutch suffered greatly under Nazi control. *Arbeitseinsatz* was imposed on the Netherlands, which obliged every man between the ages of eighteen and forty-five to work in the German factories, which were bombed every night by the Western **Allies**. Food and many other goods were taken out of the Netherlands to supply German troops. Over time, **rationing** became a way of controlling the people; any Dutch who violated

German laws automatically lost their food. Hiding Jews was even more dangerous, as it was punishable by death; as a result, one-third of the Dutch people who hid Jews did not survive the war.

These harsh measures helped feed the growth of the Dutch resistance movement, where many brave Dutch operated in secret against the Nazis.

Resistance activities included the hiding of Jews and other endangered people, such as Allied soldiers and airmen who were stranded behind enemy lines; the collection of intelligence about Nazi troop movements and supply lines; and the publication of newspapers with news from abroad.

Following the Allied invasion of Normandy on D-Day, Allied forces moved quickly to liberate the

Modern-day Amsterdam

The seat of the Netherlands' government

Netherlands. A joint American and British operation, code named "Operation Market-Garden," was executed in hope of liberating the Dutch. Unfortunately, losses were heavy, and the Allies were unable to cross the Rhine River. The end result was that the region south of the river was liberated by September of 1944, while the rest of the country had to wait until the German surrender in May 1945. That winter is known as the "hunger winter" because of the large number of Dutch who starved.

THE NETHERLANDS TODAY

The postwar years marked a period of tremendous change and growth for the Netherlands. Two days after the surrender of Japan, most of the Dutch East Indies declared its independence as Indonesia. Although it was initially thought that the loss of the territory would lead to an economic downfall, the reverse proved to be true, and in the decades that followed, the Dutch economy experienced unprecedented growth.

The rapid economic growth of the postwar period was critical to the development of the Dutch society of today. The small country soon had difficulty meeting the increased labor needs of its robust economy and began encouraging immigration as a way to meet these needs.

The postwar years were also a time of great social and cultural changes. Although the nation has been largely **homogeneous** for most of its history, today the Netherlands is a truly multicultural society as a result of immigration from countries such as Turkey and Morocco, as well as from former colonies in Asia, Africa, and the Caribbean. In the face of the challenges posed by life in the twentieth century, the changes in Dutch culture that evolved from mass immigration, and the expansion of popular culture, traditional sources of authority began to be of less importance. Young people, students in particular, rejected traditional morals, and pushed for change in matters like women's rights, sexuality, and environmental issues. Today, the Netherlands is regarded as a very liberal country, with **pragmatic** policies on matters such as drug use and prostitution and legalized **euthanasia**. Same-sex marriage became legal in 2001.

Following the struggles of World War II, the Netherlands decided to pursue a more prominent place in world affairs. Shortly after the war's end, the Netherlands sought a series of political and economic alliances. The Benelux Economic Union was signed in 1944 between Belgium, the Netherlands, and Luxembourg, and it came into effect in 1948 to promote the free movement of workers, capital, services, and goods in the region. It was the earliest **precursor** to the European Union (EU), though other organizations that led to the development of the EU were founded later (the ECSC in 1951 and the EEC in 1957). The three Benelux countries were also founding members of these intermediate organizations, together with West Germany, France, and Italy.

A modern, industrialized nation, the Netherlands is also an active member of the United Nations. The country was a founding member of NATO and adopted the euro in 2001. In recent years, the Dutch have often been a driving force behind the integration of more Central and Eastern European countries in the EU.

The Netherlands has some of the most sophisticated farms in the world.

3 THE ECONOMY

At the present time, the Dutch economy appears to be struggling out of a slight *recession*. The Netherlands is known for its open economy, which is heavily dependent on foreign trade. The country is noted for stable labor relations, moderate unemployment and inflation, a sizable current account surplus, and its critical role as a European transportation and shipping hub. The Netherlands, along with eleven other

EU members, began circulating the euro currency in 2002. Despite the current economic downturn, the country continues to be one of the leading European nations for attracting foreign direct investment.

A Social Market Economy

The long-term success of the Dutch economy is largely due to its structure as a social market economy. A social market economy has both material (financial) and social (human) dimensions.

The two main components of a market economy are **entrepreneurial** responsibility and competition. It is an entrepreneur's responsibility to see to her company's growth and to ensure that it can adapt to changing circumstances. Competition ensures that new products and technologies will constantly be developed as each business works to ensure that their product best meets the needs of the consumer. The government's role is limited to creating conditions favorable to a healthy economy by contributing to the **infrastructure**, as well as fair labor and tax laws. The government also provides assistance to those unable to cope with the greater demands of a competitive market.

The New Economy

As is happening in many industrialized nations, a shift has been made away from manufacturing as the primary source of economic growth. Although more than one-third of the Netherlands' **gross domestic product (GDP)** still comes from its

manufacturing enterprises, the dominant source of Denmark's income today comes from the **service sector**, which contributes 50 percent of the country's GDP. The largest service industry is trade, followed by transportation and telecommunications, construction, banking and insurance, and other financial services. The two largest banks are ABN Amro and ING, which operate worldwide, serving Dutch and foreign businesses and governments.

The Netherlands is an important center for multinational businesses. Its benefits include an advanced infrastructure for telecommunications and goods and passenger transport. In addition, many foreign companies come to the Netherlands because of its central geographic location, its flexible working hours, and its educated, multilingual workforce. The port of Rotterdam and Schiphol airport are the two most important international transportation hubs. Many Dutch companies have subsidiaries in other countries.

Industry: The Mainstay of Economy and Exports

Heavy industry is still an important part of the Dutch economy. More than a third of the country's GDP is dependent on the export of manufactured goods. The Dutch manufacturing sector has a broad international outlook. Dutch manufacturers

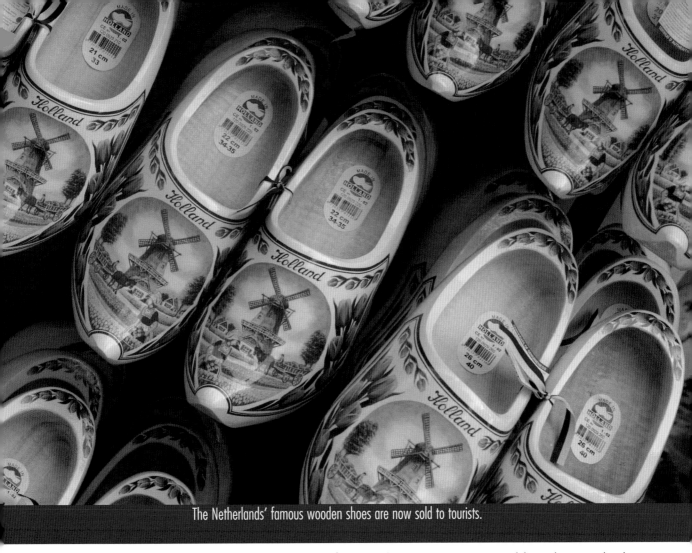

The Netherlands' famous wooden shoes are now sold to tourists.

export all over the world, have branches in many countries, and often form alliances with foreign companies. The primary manufacturing industries are chemicals, food processing, and metalworking. There are also highly developed printing and electrical engineering enterprises. Production processes in all these industries have been largely **automated** in the past ten years, making them strongly competitive on world markets, with plants both in the Netherlands and abroad.

The Netherlands is home to the world's largest chemical companies. The Dutch metalworking industry specializes in building machinery. The advanced electronic control systems have the Dutch world leaders in the manufacture of vehicles, food-processing equipment and machinery

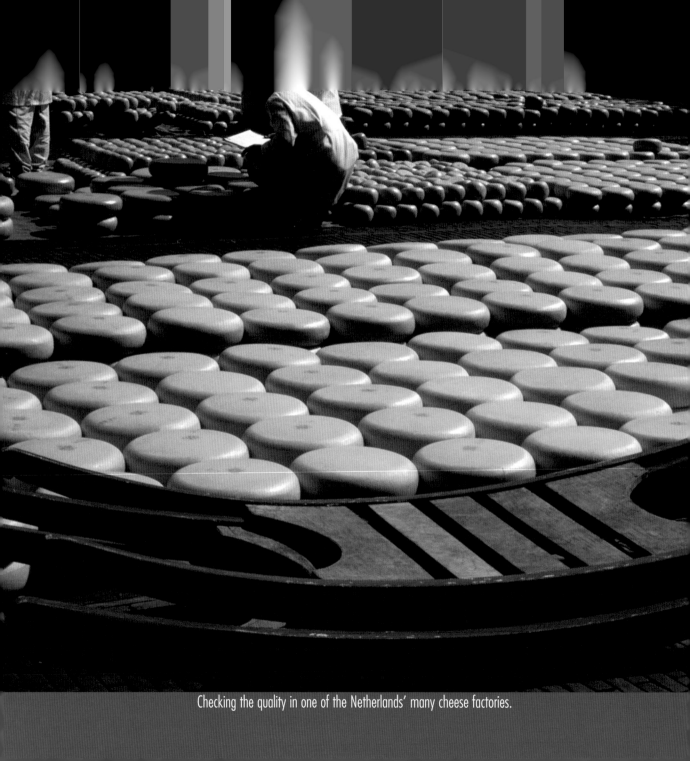

Checking the quality in one of the Netherlands' many cheese factories.

for the chemical industry. This has also promoted the growth of a thriving electronics industry. The main markets for Dutch manufactured goods are Germany, France, Belgium, and Britain. The Netherlands is the second-largest supplier of industrial equipment and consumer goods to these very demanding markets. Germany imports more from the Netherlands than from either the United States or Britain.

AGRICULTURE

Agricultural practices in the Netherlands are among the most sophisticated and environmentally sound in the world. High labor costs are constantly pushing the agriculture sector in the Netherlands to further automate production processes. For several decades, environmental legislation has also been forcing the sector to come up with cleaner and smarter products and systems.

Today's Dutch farmer is a manager. He runs his business using the data generated for him every day by sophisticated computer systems. His cows are milked by robots, which keep precise records of their production. One look at a computer screen makes it easy to see that the temperature of the milk produced by one of his cows is not quite right, or that they are not producing enough milk. The farmer then has a series of diagnostic programs to help him identify

and correct the problem. Agricultural technology has changed the face of farming forever.

As a small country, the Netherlands faces specific problems, particularly in relation to environmental protection. One problem that the Dutch have addressed successfully is the reduction of ammonia gases emitted by manure. Ammonia produced by manure is a major source of air pollution. The manure therefore has to be worked into the soil with purpose-built vehicles. In the field of animal housing technology, special grid floors and air-conditioning systems have been developed to prevent excessive concentrations of ammonia entering the environment. The Dutch have been so successful in developing agricultural technology that these systems have become important as technology and goods for export. For example, three of the four milking systems used worldwide were developed in the Netherlands.

ENERGY

Giant natural gas reserves lie in the northern area of the Netherlands, making it Western Europe's largest producer. Drilling companies operate gas and oil fields both on land and in the North Sea. The port of Rotterdam is a crucial link in Western Europe's energy supply chain. Large quantities of crude oil arrive there by ship for distribution throughout the region. The port has many refineries and terminals, and pipelines transport crude oil and oil-based products directly to the industrial centers of Germany and Belgium.

The presence of refineries and offshore installations has led to a wide range of activities serving the oil and gas industries. Four large steel construction firms, for instance, design and build entire refineries and offshore installations. Dozens of other Dutch companies produce other related equipment. Several Dutch research institutions have laboratories that simulate offshore conditions.

In recent years, the Netherlands' government has introduced strict environmental legislation. This encouraged researchers to develop technologies for purifying wastewater, neutralizing waste gases, and processing industrial and domestic pollutants. Dutch manufacturing plants are now among the world's cleanest. Around forty Dutch companies are currently making electricity generators driven by alternative energy sources such as **biomass**, sunlight, or wind. Two percent of the nation's electricity now comes from these renewable sources. The goal is to increase that to at least 10 percent by 2020.

TRANSPORTATION

The Netherlands is the hub of a complex transportation network, comprising air, sea, river, highway, and rail links extending in all directions. Rotterdam is the world's largest port, and millions of tons of cargo are loaded and unloaded there every day. Schiphol International Airport is the fourth-largest passenger and cargo airport in Europe. The Netherlands accounts for 53 percent of all the river transport on the Rhine and the Maas, and nearly a third of all European trucks make use of Dutch highways.

WORKING FOR A BRIGHTER FUTURE

The Netherlands is a country with few natural resources. As a result it has had to create wealth primarily by developing and applying knowledge.

Such collaboration is known as the "Polder Model" and refers to the way the Dutch have applied their knowledge and worked together to reclaim land from the sea. The same dedication can be seen in the way the Dutch approach research and development of new technology.

More than 60,000 researchers work in Dutch companies, universities, and research institutes. These researchers produce 7 percent of the EU's scientific publications and hold 6 percent of its patents. Several development projects for the knowledge infrastructure are currently in progress, with more than two hundred million euros in funding allocated for this work. These projects are forging connections between companies, educational institutions, and government in areas such as **miniaturization**, **hydraulic engineering** in delta areas, traffic and transport, biotechnology, and data communications.

As the Dutch look toward the future, they are hopeful that this continued investment into research and new technology will help create not only a stronger economy and more prosperous country, but a cleaner and safer world.

Dutch vendors

Dutch culture is built around
its lowlying land and canals.

CHAPTER 4

THE NETHERLANDS' PEOPLE AND CULTURE

The Netherlands, home to over 16 million people, is one of the world's most densely populated countries. The tiny country has more than 1,000 inhabitants per square mile (more than 460 inhabitants per square kilometer). There are two official languages, Dutch and Frisian, both Germanic languages. Frisian is only spoken in the northern province of Friesland; it is the language that most closely resembles English

According to local tradition, it is said that farmers from the north of England can converse with their Frisian counterparts about their shared livelihoods without difficulty.

Ethnic minorities make up 9 percent of the Netherlands' population. Immigrants, mostly from Turkey, Morocco, and Italy, account for most of these minority groups. Many of these immigrants have assimilated Dutch language and culture, assisted by the ability of minority communities to obtain government funding to set up their own schools. It is possible, therefore, for a Moroccan child living in the Netherlands to attend a publicly funded school where her lessons are taught in both Dutch and Arabic.

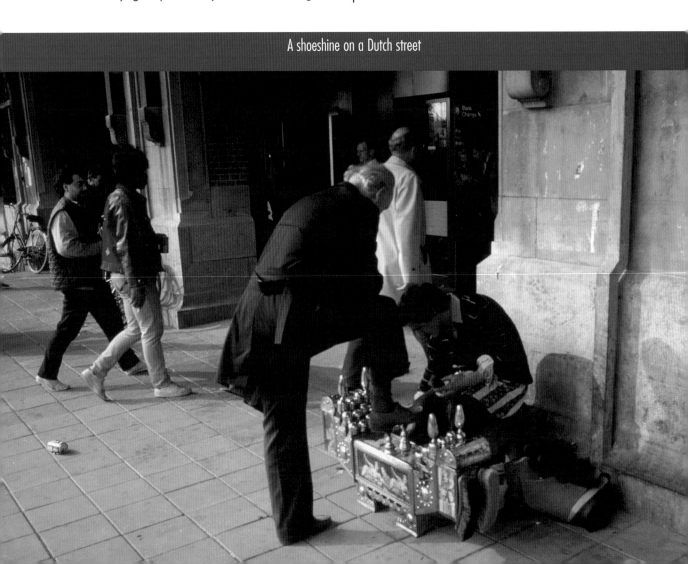

A shoeshine on a Dutch street

Religion: Freedom of Choice

The Dutch people have full freedom to choose their faith and religion. The Netherlands is now one of the most **secular** countries in Europe; an estimated 40 percent of the population is nonreligious. The remaining are 31 percent Roman Catholic, 21 percent Protestant, and nearly 5 percent Muslim. Protestants used to be the largest religious group in the Netherlands, but over the past century, the older Protestant churches have seen a rapid decline. Islam has begun to gain foothold in recent years, due in large part to the large number of immigrants from the Middle East.

Food and Drink: Simple Fare

In the Netherlands it is common to have two cold meals and one hot meal a day. Bread, fruit, and cheese are generally eaten with breakfast and lunch. Sometimes crisp bread, crackers, rye bread, or cereal flakes called muesli are substituted for the bread. Dinner usually begins with soup, and the main course consists of boiled potatoes, vegetables, and roasted meat or fish. Rice, other grains, or pasta sometimes take the place of the potatoes. Dessert is usually yogurt, cold custard, or fruit.

The Netherlands is famous for its dairy products, especially its cheeses. Traditional Dutch cheeses include Gouda, Edam, and Leyden.

Education: A Literate People

It is compulsory for children in the Netherlands to attend school full time from the age of five, and many attend school part time between the ages of sixteen and eighteen. The content taught in all types of schools is established by law, as are goals for proficiency. This enables the government to ensure that education standards are uniform throughout the country.

Schools set up by local governments are called public-authority schools. All other schools, founded by private bodies, are called private schools. Though more than three-quarters of the schools in the Netherlands are private, they are all eligible for government funding, provided they meet some basic criteria. Teachers are also paid by the government. In 2001, the Netherlands spent more than 5 percent of its GDP on education. Education is free of charge for children up to the age of sixteen.

Primary schools in the Netherlands cater to children from ages four to twelve. The eight-year primary school curriculum focuses on pupils' emotional, intellectual, and artistic development, along with the acquisition of essential social, cultural, and physical skills. At the age of twelve, children are separated into one of three different kinds of schools: prevocational secondary school, which takes four years to complete; general secondary school, which takes five years to complete; or pre-

university school, which takes six years to complete. Parents of students between the ages of sixteen and eighteen are required to pay for textbooks and other teaching materials. This is offset by the child benefit all Dutch parents receive from the government for children under the age of eighteen.

Students eighteen or older have to pay for their education. Fees for most university courses are the same. All students over eighteen receive a basic government grant, which they may supplement with a loan. The amount of the loan will depend on the student's income. The student's academic achievement also plays a role. The Dutch government invests heavily in education, and as a result, the Dutch people are highly literate, and many are fluent in more than one language.

QUICK FACTS: THE PEOPLE OF THE NETHERLANDS

Population: 16,407,491
Age structure:
  0–14 years: 18.1%
  15–64 years: 67.8%
  65 years and over: 14.1%
Population growth rate: 0.53%
Birth rate: 11.14 births/1,000 population
Death rate: 8.68 deaths/1,000 population
Migration rate: 2.8 migrant(s)/1,000 population
Infant mortality rate: 5.04 deaths/1,000 live births
Life expectancy at birth:
  total population: 78.81 years
  male: 76.25 years
  female: 81.51 years
Total fertility rate: 1.66 children born/woman
Religions: Roman Catholic 31%, Dutch Reformed 13%, Calvinist 7%, Muslim 5.5%, ither 2.5%, none 41% (2002)
Languages: Dutch (official), Frisian (official)
Literacy: total population: 99% (2000)

Note: All figures are from 2005 unless otherwise noted.
Source: www.cia.gov, 2005.

FESTIVALS AND EVENTS: A FUN-LOVING PEOPLE

The Dutch really know how to celebrate a holiday. Parades, costume parties, crowded streets, floats, shows, and dances—the Dutch love a good party.

While the country only observes eight public holidays nationwide, many festivals and events are celebrated on a regional or national scale. These celebrations may be religious or secular in nature. One Dutch tradition that should be familiar to American children is *Sinterklaas*, celebrated on December 5.

Cheese carriers in a Dutch village

A sign for "stork delivery" in a Netherlands town

There are some distinctions between Sinterklaas, and Santa Claus, however. Santa lives at the North Pole, while Dutch children know Sinterklaas is making his list of naughty and nice children on the sunny coast of Spain. Santa has an army of elves for helpers, while Sinterklaas has large, black-faced helpers called the *Zwarte Pieten*. Sinterklaas, as the legend goes, arrives in the Netherlands by steamer from his home in Spain a couple of weeks before his birthday. His arrival occurs at a designated port city each year, and the parade that follows is broadcast on national television. Actors dressed as the Saint and his black helpers enter town in large, colorful processions. The Saint rides a white horse, and his helpers poke fun at bystanders while throwing small ginger biscuits at them. Sinterklaas sightings are then common over the next several days. Finally, on December 5, children put their shoes by the fireplace in hopes that Sinterklaas will fill them with treats, assuming they have been good over the previous year. Bad children can expect to be deported to Spain by the Zwarte Pieten in the middle of the night.

Some controversy has developed in recent years over the black face worn by actors impersonating the Zwarte Pieten. Some say this tradition reflects the soot the helpers picked up from the chimneys they went down. Others think they represent the feared Moors of old Spain, who were considered evil enough to frighten any medieval Dutch child into behaving. Some today people feel the blacking-up should stop as it represents an unacceptable racial stereotype. The picture of mischievous, black servants carrying out the wishes of a good, white master is distasteful to some observers, although most Dutch people still feel it is a harmless tradition. Nonetheless, whether the black makeup stays or goes, the feast of Sinterklaas is a shining example of the enthusiasm with which the Dutch celebrate their holidays.

ARTS AND ARCHITECTURE

The height of Dutch architecture was during the seventeenth century. Due to the thriving economy, Dutch cities expanded greatly during this period. New town halls, weighing houses, and storehouses were built. Merchants with newly obtained fortunes ordered houses built along one of the many new canals that were dug out in and around many cities. Many of these homes with their grand façades can still be seen and appreciated.

The Netherlands has produced many great artists over the centuries. From the paintings of Rembrandt van Rijn and Johannes Vermeer in the seventeenth century, to the genius of Vincent van Gogh in the nineteenth century, to the more modern works of Piet Mondrian and M. C. Escher, the Dutch have a proud artistic tradition.

One of Amsterdam's many canals

5 CHAPTER THE CITIES

The Netherlands is an extremely urban society. More than 80 percent of its population lives in cities and towns. Most Dutch citizens earn a fairly comfortable income and lead prosperous lifestyles. Because land is at a premium, Dutch cities tend to be densely populated industrial centers, as most open land is reserved for agriculture. Nonetheless, the high population density and level of industrialization cannot diminish the appeal of these ancient cities, brimming with important architecture, cultural attractions, and significant historical sites.

AMSTERDAM: THE CAPITAL

Amsterdam is the capital of the Netherlands. Founded in the late twelfth century as a small fishing village on the banks of the Amstel River, it is now the nation's largest city and its financial and cultural center. As of 2005, the population of the greater Amsterdam area is approximately one and a half million. The old city was built up around a series of concentric, semicircular canals, which still define the city's layout and appearance. Many fine examples of Dutch architecture can be found among the houses and mansions situated along these canals; most are lived in, others are now offices, and some are public buildings.

Today, the city is noted for many outstanding museums, including the Rijksmuseum, the Van Gogh Museum, the Stedelijk Museum, Rembrandt House Museum, the Anne Frank House, and its world-class symphony orchestra. It also has a quite different reputation for its red-light district, de Wallen, and the many coffee shops where marijuana is legally available.

DELFT: HOME OF WILLIAM OF ORANGE

Delft was granted a city charter in 1246, and original medieval structures of that period are still recognizable in the old city center. The town developed into a vibrant commercial town thanks to its textile industries, breweries, and shipping trade. In 1536, a major fire almost destroyed the town. Shortly afterward, it became the residence of the princes of Orange, Holland's royal family. William of Orange was living in Delft when he was murdered, and the bullet holes from the attack are still visible in the present Municipal Museum. The prince's marble mausoleum can be admired in the New Church, over the vault of the royal family. The collection of the Military Museum in the old armory shows the military history of the House of Orange.

Delft is renowned all over the world as the birthplace of Delft Blue pottery. In the seventeenth century, dozens of small pottery factories arose in Delft in buildings that formerly housed breweries. Delft was one of the homeports of the Dutch East India Company, and when the Delft potters became acquainted with imported Chinese porcelain, they began manufacturing Delftware with designs based on these patterns, which is still made by hand today.

MAASTRICHT: A SUNNY RETREAT

The southernmost and sunniest city in the Netherlands, Maastricht, is a beautiful walled city of Roman origin set on the river Maas. The green, unspoiled hillsides that surround Maastricht are home to famous vineyards and provide the opportunity for many kinds of outdoor recreation. Architecture and history enthusiasts will not be disappointed either, since Maastricht has an abundance of ramparts, caves, tunnels, grottos, museums, and basilicas to explore.

THE HAGUE: A ROYAL CITY

The history of The Hague begins in the thirteenth century when the site was chosen as the ideal place for a hunting lodge by the counts of Holland. The elaborate hunting lodge drew other nobles who built their own grand houses, and a village for traders and craftsmen soon developed. In 1248, William II, Count of Holland, began the construction of a castle on the Binnenhof. William's son, Floris V, added the massive Knights' Hall, expanding a complex that today is the seat of the country's administrative government.

Rotterdam is a modern city.

Today, The Hague is not only the official seat of government, it is also the home of the Dutch royal family. If the flag is raised at Huis Ten Bosch Palace, Queen Beatrix and Prince Claus are in residence. The queen has her offices in Noordeinde Palace, in the city center. Each year, on the third Tuesday of September, the royal family rides in a golden coach to the Binnenhof. Queen Beatrix also officially opens the new parliamentary year by making her annual address from the throne at the Ridderzaal.

Over the centuries, The Hague has grown into a cosmopolitan city; it now boasts no fewer than three royal palaces, more than sixty foreign embassies, and the headquarters for innumerable international engineering, oil, and chemical con-

cerns. The lush greenery of the original hunting grounds can still be seen in the large parks, gardens, and woods that continue to thrive within the city limits.

The Hague is perhaps best known as the International City of Peace and Justice. The International Criminal Court, the Peace Palace, the War Crimes Tribunal, and Europol are all headquartered here.

ROTTERDAM: THE WORLD'S LARGEST HARBOR CITY

Rotterdam derives its name from the Rotte River. In the thirteenth century, a fishing village was built near a dam in the Rotte. The village was granted a municipal charter in 1340 and grew into a prosperous trading town during the sixteenth and seventeenth centuries, with many warehouses and shipyards. By the late nineteenth, century, Rotterdam had developed into an international center of trade, transport, and industry.

The town's center, as well as the harbor, was completely destroyed by German bombers on May 14, 1940. In the years following the war, every effort was made to reconstruct the city. In the 1960s, Rotterdam achieved its status as the world's largest harbor, a distinction it still holds. Meanwhile, a new city center was constructed with cosmopolitan appeal. This reconstruction has given Rotterdam its unique architectural char-

acter. A new inner city developed, with modern and functional architecture oriented toward the river, and a series of experiments in city planning have earned admiration from visitors from around the world.

UTRECHT: A CENTER OF LEARNING

Utrecht is almost 2,000 years old. It all began with a Roman fortification established in 47 BCE as part of the reinforcements along the Rhine River against invasions from Germania. In 1122, Utrecht was granted a city charter, and the city's historic canals and wharves date from this period. For centuries, Utrecht was the only city of importance in the north of Holland. Utrecht played a major role during the Eighty Years' War against Spain. In 1579, the famed Union of Utrecht was formed in the large chapter house, which is now the university auditorium. This was a beginning to the northern provinces' **secession** from Spanish rule, which led to the formation of the powerful Republic of the Seven United Netherlands, the first republic in postmedieval Europe. Additional growth came in 1636 with the founding of the university.

Today Utrecht is a bustling university city, brimming with museums, theaters, and historic finds. The city has prospered thanks to its favorable location in the heart of the Netherlands. The city lies at the crossroads for transportation, art, knowledge, service, and commerce.

The EU flag

6 THE FORMATION OF THE EUROPEAN UNION

CHAPTER

The EU is an economic and political confederation of twenty-five European nations. Member countries abide by common foreign and security policies and cooperate on judicial and domestic affairs. The confederation, however, does not replace existing states or governments. Each of the twenty-five member states is **autonomous**, but they have all agreed to establish some common institutions and to hand over some of their own decision-making powers to these international bodies. As a result, decisions on matters that interest all member states can be made democratically, accommodating everyone's concerns and interests.

Today, the EU is the most powerful regional organization in the world. It has evolved from a primarily economic organization to an increasingly political one. Besides promoting economic cooperation, the EU requires that its members uphold fundamental values of peace and **_solidarity_**, human dignity, freedom, and equality. Based on the principles of democracy and the rule of law, the EU respects the culture and organizations of member states.

HISTORY

The seeds of the EU were planted more than fifty years ago in a Europe reduced to smoking piles of rubble by two world wars. European nations suffered great financial difficulties in the postwar period. They were struggling to get back on their feet and realized that another war would cause further hardship. Knowing that internal conflict was hurting all of Europe, a drive began toward European cooperation.

France took the first historic step. On May 9, 1950 (now celebrated as Europe Day), Robert Schuman, the French foreign minister, proposed the coal and steel industries of France and West Germany be coordinated under a single supranational authority. The proposal, known as the Treaty

of Paris, attracted four other countries—Belgium, Luxembourg, the Netherlands, and Italy—and resulted in the 1951 formation of the European Coal and Steel Community (ECSC). These six countries became the founding members of the EU.

In 1957, European cooperation took its next big leap. Under the Treaty of Rome, the European Economic Community (EEC) and the European Atomic Energy Community (EURATOM) were formed. Informally known as the Common Market, the EEC promoted joining the national economies into a single European economy. The 1965 Treaty of Brussels (more commonly referred to as the Merger Treaty) united these various treaty organizations under a single umbrella, the European Community (EC).

In 1992, the Maastricht Treaty (also known as the Treaty of the European Union) was signed in Maastricht, the Netherlands, signaling the birth of the EU as it stands today. **_Ratified_** the following year, the Maastricht Treaty provided f banking system, a common currency (replace the national currencies, a leg of the EU, and a framework for exp

The EU's united economy has allowed it to become a worldwide financial power.

EU's political role, particularly in the area of foreign and security policy.

By 1993, the member countries completed their move toward a single market and agreed to participate in a larger common market, the European Economic Area, established in 1994.

The EU, headquartered in Brussels, Belgium, reached its current member strength in spurts. In

© BCE ECB EZB EKT EKP 2002

© BCE ECB EZB EKT EKP 2002

© BCE ECB EZB EKT EKP 2002

© BCE ECB EZB EKT EKP 2002

1973, Denmark, Ireland, and the United Kingdom joined the six founding members of the EC. They were followed by Greece in 1981, and Portugal and Spain in 1986. The 1990s saw the unification of the two Germanys, and as a result, East Germany entered the EU fold. Austria, Finland, and Sweden joined the EU in 1995, bringing the total number of member states to fifteen. In 2004, the EU nearly doubled its size when ten countries—Cyprus, the Czech Republic, Estonia, Hungary, Latvia, Lithuania, Malta, Poland, Slovakia, and Slovenia—became members.

The EU Framework

The EU's structure has often been compared to a "roof of a temple with three columns." As established by the Maastricht Treaty, this three-pillar framework encompasses all the policy areas—or pillars—of European cooperation. The three pillars of the EU are the European Community, the Common Foreign and Security Policy (CFSP), and Police and Judicial Co-operation in Criminal Matters.

Quick Facts: The European Union

Number of Member Countries: 25

Official Languages: 20—Czech, Danish, Dutch, English, Estonian, Finnish, French, German, Greek, Hungarian, Italian, Latvian, Lithuanian, Maltese, Polish, Portuguese, Slovak, Slovenian, Spanish, and Swedish; additional language for treaty purposes: Irish Gaelic

Motto: *In Varietate Concordia* (United in Diversity)

European Council's President: Each member state takes a turn to lead the council's activities for 6 months.

European Commission's President: José Manuel Barroso (Portugal)

European Parliament's President: Josep Borrell (Spain)

Total Area: 1,502,966 square miles (3,892,685 sq. km.)

Population: 454,900,000

Population Density: 302.7 people/square mile (116.8 people/sq. km.)

GDP: €9.61.1012

Per Capita GDP: €21,125

Formation:
- Declared: February 7, 1992, with signing of the Maastricht Treaty
- Recognized: November 1, 1993, with the ratification of the Maastricht Treaty

Community Currency: Euro. Currently 12 of the 25 member states have adopted the euro as their currency.

Anthem: "Ode to Joy"

Flag: Blue background with 12 gold stars arranged in a circle

Official Day: Europe Day, May 9

Source: europa.eu.int

Pillar One

The European Community pillar deals with economic, social, and environmental policies. It is a body consisting of the European Parliament, European Commission, European Court of Justice, Council of the European Union, and the European Courts of Auditors.

Pillar Two

The idea that the EU should speak with one voice in world affairs is as old as the European integration process itself. Toward this end, the Common Foreign and Security Policy (CFSP) was formed in 1993.

PILLAR THREE

The cooperation of EU member states in judicial and criminal matters ensures that its citizens enjoy the freedom to travel, work, and live securely and safely anywhere within the EU. The third pillar—Police and Judicial Co-operation in Criminal Matters—helps to protect EU citizens from international crime and to ensure equal access to justice and fundamental rights across the EU.

The flags of the EU's nations:

top row, left to right
Belgium, the Czech Republic, Denmark, Germany, Estonia, Greece

second row, left to right
Spain, France, Ireland, Italy, Cyprus, Latvia

third row, left to right
Lithuania, Luxembourg, Hungary, Malta, the Netherlands, Austria

bottom row, left to right
Poland, Portugal, Slovenia, Slovakia, Finland, Sweden, United Kingdom

ECONOMIC STATUS

As of May 2004, the EU had the largest economy in the world, followed closely by the United States. But even though the EU continues to enjoy a trade surplus, it faces the twin problems of high unemployment rates and **stagnancy**.

The 2004 addition of ten new member states is expected to boost economic growth. EU membership is likely to stimulate the economies of these relatively poor countries. In turn, their prosperity growth will be beneficial to the EU.

THE EURO

The EU's official currency is the euro, which came into circulation on January 1, 2002. The shift to the euro has been the largest monetary changeover in the world. Twelve countries—Belgium, Germany, Greece, Spain, France, Ireland, Italy, Luxembourg, the Netherlands, Finland, Portugal, and Austria—have adopted it as their currency.

SINGLE MARKET

Within the EU, laws of member states are harmonized and domestic policies are coordinated to create a larger, more-efficient single market.

The chief features of the EU's internal policy on the single market are:

- free trade of goods and services

- a common EU competition law that controls anticompetitive activities of companies and member states

- removal of internal border control and harmonization of external controls between member states

- freedom for citizens to live and work anywhere in the EU as long as they are not dependent on the state

- free movement of **capital** between member states

- harmonization of government regulations, corporation law, and trademark registration

- a single currency

- coordination of environmental policy

- a common agricultural policy and a common fisheries policy

- a common system of indirect taxation, the value-added tax (VAT), and common customs duties and **excise**

- funding for research

- funding for aid to disadvantaged regions

The EU's external policy on the single market specifies:

- a common external **tariff** and a common position in international trade negotiations

- funding of programs in other Eastern European countries and developing countries

COOPERATION AREAS

EU member states cooperate in other areas as well. Member states can vote in European Parliament elections. Intelligence sharing and cooperation in criminal matters are carried out through EUROPOL and the Schengen Information System.

The EU is working to develop common foreign and security policies. Many member states are resisting such a move, however, saying these are sensitive areas best left to individual member states. Arguing in favor of a common approach to security and foreign policy are countries like France and Germany, who insist that a safer and more secure Europe can only become a reality under the EU umbrella.

One of the EU's great achievements has been to create a boundary-free area within which people, goods, services, and money can move around freely; this ease of movement is sometimes called "the four freedoms." As the EU grows in size, so do the challenges facing it—and yet its fifty-year history has amply demonstrated the power of cooperation.

Europe is proud of its "bright idea," a union with economic and political power.

The EU believes that it can use its power to act as a "lighthouse" for the rest of the world.

KEY EU INSTITUTIONS

Five key institutions play a specific role in the EU.

THE EUROPEAN PARLIAMENT

The European Parliament (EP) is the democratic voice of the people of Europe. Directly elected every five years, the Members of the European Parliament (MEPs) sit not in national **blocs** but in political groups representing the seven main political parties of the member states. Each group reflects the political ideology of the national parties to which its members belong. Some MEPs are not attached to any political group.

COUNCIL OF THE EUROPEAN UNION

The Council of the European Union (formerly known as the Council of Ministers) is the main legislative and decision-making body in the EU. It brings together the nationally elected representatives of the member-state governments. One minister from each of the EU's member states attends council meetings. It is the forum in which government representatives can assert their interests and reach compromises. Increasingly, the Council of the European Union and the EP are acting together as colegislators in decision-making processes.

European Commission

The European Commission does much of the day-to-day work of the EU. Politically independent, the commission represents the interests of the EU as a whole, rather than those of individual member states. It drafts proposals for new European laws, which it presents to the EP and the Council of the European Union. The European Commission makes sure EU decisions are implemented properly and supervises the way EU funds are spent. It also sees that everyone abides by the European treaties and European law.

The EU member-state governments choose the European Commission president, who is then approved by the EP. Member states, in consultation with the incoming president, nominate the other European Commission members, who must also be approved by the EP. The commission is appointed for a five-year term, but can be dismissed by the EP. Many members of its staff work in Brussels, Belgium.

Court of Justice

Headquartered in Luxembourg, the Court of Justice of the European Communities consists of one independent judge from each EU country. This court ensures that the common rules decided in the EU are understood and followed uniformly by all the members. The Court of Justice settles disputes over how EU treaties and legislation are interpreted. If national courts are in doubt about how to apply EU rules, they must ask the Court of Justice. Individuals can also bring proceedings against EU institutions before the court.

Court of Auditors

EU funds must be used legally, economically, and for their intended purpose. The Court of Auditors, an independent EU institution located in Luxembourg, is responsible for overseeing how EU money is spent. In effect, these auditors help European taxpayers get better value for the money that has been channeled into the EU.

Other Important Bodies

1. European Economic and Social Committee: expresses the opinions of organized civil society on economic and social issues

2. Committee of the Regions: expresses the opinions of regional and local authorities

3. European Central Bank: responsible for monetary policy and managing the euro

4. European Ombudsman: deals with citizens' complaints about mismanagement by any EU institution or body

5. European Investment Bank: helps achieve EU objectives by financing investment projects

Together with a number of agencies and other bodies completing the system, the EU's institutions have made it the most powerful organization in the world.

EU MEMBER STATES

In order to become a member of the EU, a country must have a stable democracy that guarantees the rule of law, human rights, and protection of minorities. It must also have a functioning market economy as well as a civil service capable of applying and managing EU laws.

The EU provides substantial financial assistance and advice to help candidate countries prepare themselves for membership. As of October 2004, the EU has twenty-five member states. Bulgaria and Romania are likely to join in 2007, which would bring the EU's total population to nearly 500 million.

In December 2004, the EU decided to open negotiations with Turkey on its proposed membership. Turkey's possible entry into the EU has been fraught with controversy. Much of this controversy has centered on Turkey's human rights record and the divided island of Cyprus. If allowed to join the EU, Turkey would be its most-populous member state.

The 2004 expansion was the EU's most ambitious enlargement to date. Never before has the EU embraced so many new countries, grown so much in terms of area and population, or encompassed so many different histories and cultures. As the EU moves forward into the twenty-first century, it will undoubtedly continue to grow in both political and economic strength.

The Dutch flag

7 THE NETHERLANDS IN THE EUROPEAN UNION

The Netherlands regards the EU as a network to provide security, democracy, and economic prosperity. As a founding member of the European Economic Community, the Netherlands has long played a critical role in promoting EU integration and in developing closer European ties. EU policies, driven by common rather than national interests, offers protection to smaller countries such as the

The Netherlands in EU History

The Benelux Economic Union, signed in 1944 between Belgium, the Netherlands, and Luxembourg, came into effect in 1948 to promote the free movement of workers, capital, services, and goods in the region. It was the earliest precursor to the EU, though other organizations that led to the development of the EU were founded later. These included the European Coal and Steel Community in 1951 and the European Economic Community or EEC in 1957. The three Benelux countries were founding members of these intermediate organizations, together with West Germany, France, and Italy. As the EEC evolved into the EU and transformed from a trade body into an economic and political partnership, the foundation was laid for the development of the largest union in the world. Throughout the EU's history, the Dutch have played a critical role in increasing the EU's influence and strength.

Differing Views of European Cooperation

The Netherlands are central to the EU for many reasons. In addition to its central geographic location, the country has functioned politically as a driving force for European unification. It has traditionally supported greater cooperation within the EU, as well as economic and political *integration*. Many prominent Dutch politicians favor a policy known as supranationalism—a governmental approach in which EU member states would have to give up some decision-making control to appointed officials or elected representatives; decisions would be based on "majority rules." Supranationalism is heavily supported by some of the largest EU member nations, including Germany. The attempt to ratify a new European constitution, which would supersede existing national constitutions, is an outgrowth of this movement.

Britain and some of the newer EU members oppose this vision of Europe. They want to surrender a minimum of sovereignty, especially over such things as taxation, defense, and foreign affairs. They are anxious to maintain close links with the United States. They are against supranationalism, instead favoring intergovernmentalism—a governmental approach in which member states must reach unanimous agreement before moving ahead on decisions.

Recent events have shown that whatever the feelings of the politicians, the Dutch voting public is in no hurry to surrender additional sovereignty to the EU. More than 60 percent of Dutch voters defeated a proposal to adopt the EU constitution in a *referendum* held in 2005. Polls showed that the Dutch feared for their national interests as the EU expanded, and they were unwilling to surrender their cherished policies on issues like prostitution, euthanasia, same-sex marriage, and legalized marijuana in deference to the policies of a greater Europe.

A Balancing Act

As an EU member, the Netherlands has had to concede some of its rights. Although the country has its own laws and rules, it is so closely tied to the EU that it is no longer able to act independently in many areas.

For instance, the Netherlands no longer acts alone in international economic matters. Now it usually acts through Europe. The Netherlands also increasingly makes its international policies in conjunction and consultation with other EU members.

The challenge for today's Netherlands is to strike the right balance between domestic and EU responsibilities. Take for example the Netherland's welfare policy. The Netherlands has always had a generous social welfare policy toward its unemployed. This welfare policy places a great strain on the country's finances. Though the country is willing to bear the financial burden, it is under pressure from the EU to trim its budget. However, the

Railway bridge in Dordrecht

country won't compromise by reducing welfare programs.

LOBBYING FOR LOWER TRADE BARRIERS

The Netherlands is one of Europe's largest trading nations, and a majority of Dutch jobs depend on foreign trade. The country's economy has traditionally been driven by exports, since Dutch factories have always produced more than could be sold in the domestic market.

The country's most important trading partners are its fellow EU members, as well as the United States. Since EU members account for more than half of Dutch trade, the formation of a single market has greatly benefited the country. Now the Dutch are supporting EU efforts to reduce trade barriers that prevent developing countries from marketing their goods in EU member countries. Currently, developing countries wanting to export their goods to EU nations have to pay taxes, which in some instances are quite high. Often, they cannot sell more than a specified amount to the EU nation, since the latter has fixed a **quota** for imports.

The Netherlands wants these trade barriers eliminated. Once they are removed, the developing countries would have to grant greater access to EU nations. This would be of advantage to the Dutch, since they need to find buyers for their excess goods.

SEEKING REFORM OF CAP

A major component of EU policy is its Common Agricultural Policy, or CAP. The program's aim is to provide farmers with a reasonable standard of living and consumers with quality food at fair prices. Today, CAP's focus is on food safety, preservation of the environment, and value for money.

Although modernization of farms, rural development, and fair payments to farmers have been the top priorities of the EU agenda, other concerns have begun to push their way forward. More intensive farming methods have sparked concerns that the environment and animal welfare are not getting the attention they deserve. Consumers feared that unsafe production meth-

ods were to blame for mad cow disease, the chemical dioxin in milk, artificial hormones in meat, and other food-related health scares. Consequently, the Dutch are demanding that CAP be reformed because of its high cost and its failure to prevent these safety crises.

The Dutch government believes that CAP reforms must be addressed through more open market access, fewer export subsidies, and less internal support that disrupts trade. They are also seeking greater accountability in matters such as food safety, animal welfare, and sustainability. All these reforms have sound scientific foundations. The Dutch have done considerable research into **sustainable** production, careful use of natural resources, and methods to control plant and animal diseases.

EU ENLARGEMENT AND DUTCH CONCERNS

The EU enlargement has created multiple difficulties for the Dutch by placing a financial burden on the country and creating competition from within the EU.

Many of the countries that joined the EU in 2004 are relatively poor compared to their Western European counterparts. Nations like Cyprus, the Czech Republic, Estonia, Hungary, Latvia, Lithuania, Malta, Poland, Slovakia, and Slovenia have small economies and relatively weak infrastructures; as a result, few world-class companies are willing to invest there.

These new member countries are turning to the EU for financial assistance in order to develop their infrastructures and raise the standard of living so that it is more in line with that enjoyed across the rest of Europe. To increase investment in their countries, they have set very low corporate tax levels to encourage foreign investors to set up offices and factories in their cities.

To provide for the needs of the new member countries, the EU has asked richer nations like the Netherlands to increase their budget contributions. Since the nation is currently in a slight recession, the demand places a great burden on that country. Although the Dutch have supported the continued enlargement of the EU, many Dutch voters now fear the additional drain this will place on their economy, already burdened by the cost of their extensive welfare programs. In addition, although the Dutch have embraced immigration in the past as a means of meeting the labor needs of their growing economy, concern now exists that the small nation will be flooded by an influx of unskilled labor from the new members of the EU, putting an even greater strain on the nation's extensive network of social services.

THE WAY FORWARD

While individual nations continue to protect their sovereignty and interests, Europeans cannot deny that the EU has greatly improved the standard of living, security, and international influence of member states. Continued efforts to set up a common customs union for all EU member states, reduce trade barriers, and adopt common quality standards for goods and services have begun to pay dividends for the Netherlands as well as the rest of Europe.

A Calendar of Dutch Festivals

The Netherlands celebrates many religious, historical, and nonreligious festivals. Food, fun, parades, and dancing are integral parts of most Dutch festivals.

January: January 1 is a public holiday. The Dutch have their own unique way of celebrating **New Year's Eve**. They stay at home and celebrate quietly with the family until midnight, then dash out on the streets and indulge in a wild display of fireworks and bonfires.

February: February is carnival month. **Carnival** takes place during the fasting period before **Lent**. Normal, everyday law gives way to the orders of the town's eleven-member Carnival Committee, whose sole goal is to stop anyone from being serious during Carnival time. Local leaders are caricatured in masks, and songs are sung poking fun at celebrities and politicians. Dutch towns hold parades consisting of grotesque, papier-mâché figures on floats and people dressed up in outrageous outfits. Brass bands blast out music as the normally conservative citizens suddenly dance the conga together through the streets. Many, many bottles of beer disappear, and TV and radio devote hours to popular (and sometimes obscene) Carnival songs. **Valentine's Day** is also celebrated in the Netherlands on February 14.

March/April: Easter Week may fall in March or April, and the festival is celebrated throughout the country. The Dutch celebrate with a four-day weekend on Easter as both Good Friday and Easter Monday are public holidays. **Women's Day** is celebrated on March 8. **Koninginnedag** or Queen's Day is held April 30 and is a national holiday. It is billed as the biggest collective street market and party in the world. The streets are filled with huge crowds of people wearing bright orange, who may be there to pick up a good bargain from the many street stalls or just to party at one of the live music events. On this day only, anyone can set up a street stall, and no one needs a license to play music in public. The queen makes two or three stops in villages across the country, often stopping at a random Dutch home to meet with ordinary people.

May: May 1 is **Dag van de arbeid**, Labor Day. **Ascension Day** and **Whit Monday**, initially observed as religious festivals, are now public holidays in May. May 4 is **War Dead Remembrance Day**, and honors those who died during World War II. May 5 is **Liberation Day**, and celebrates the final liberation of the Dutch from Nazi occupation in 1945. **Mother's Day** is celebrated on May 8.

June/July/August: The Dutch have few organized holidays during the summer months. **Father's Day** is celebrated in June. August 2 marks **Armistice Day**, celebrating the end of World War II.

September: Prince's Day, on September 20, is a patriotic holiday honoring the Dutch royal family. It is traditional to fly the Dutch flag on this day.

October: October 4 is **World Animal Day**, a number of Dutch towns honor this date with exhibits promoting animal welfare.

November: November 2 is **Thanksgiving**, a celebration to give thanks for the harvest. **Sintmaarten**, is a holiday commemorating the life of a Roman Catholic saint. On November 11, small groups of children, usually accompanied by an adult, go door to door through the streets. They hold small lanterns made from paper or turnips on sticks in front of them as they knock on doors and sing songs or recite little poems in exchange for treats of candy and fruit. Faces are carved into the turnips so the candles placed inside can shine through, not unlike the jack o'lanterns made by American children on Halloween.

December: On December 5, the eve of **Sinterklaas**, the Dutch Santa visits children. Children place their shoes by the fireplace. Good children get toys and sweets in their boots; bad ones get deported to Spain. **Christmas Day**, December 25, is family time in the Netherlands, celebrated with a special meal. The following day, December 26, is known as Boxing Day and is the traditional time for family and friends to exchange gifts.

Appelkoek
(Apple Cake)

Makes 6 servings

Ingredients
2 medium apples
1 1/2 cups flour
3 1/2 teaspoons baking powder
1/2 teaspoon salt
6 tablespoon granulated sugar, divided
1/4 cup margarine or butter
1 egg, well beaten
3/4 cup milk
1/2 teaspoon ground cinnamon

Directions
Peel and cut apples into eighths (wedges). Sift together flour, baking powder, and salt with 4 tablespoons of the sugar. Cut in butter/margarine. Combine egg and milk and add to flour mixture. Turn batter into greased 8-inch square cake pan. Press apple wedges partly into batter. Combine remaining 2 tablespoons sugar and cinnamon, sprinkle over apples. Bake at 425°F for 25 to 30 minutes.

Speculaas
(Spice Cookies)

These cookies are a favorite among school-age children.

Makes 4 to 6 dozen

Ingredients
1 cup margarine or butter
1 1/2 cups packed brown sugar
1 1/2 teaspoon ground cinnamon
1 teaspoon baking powder
1/2 teaspoon ground nutmeg
1/2 teaspoon ground cloves
1/4 teaspoon salt
1 egg
2 3/4 cups all-purpose flour
1/3 cup finely chopped blanched almonds (optional)
blanched whole almonds (optional)

Directions
Beat margarine or butter with a mixer on medium to high speed for 30 seconds or by hand. Add brown sugar, cinnamon, baking powder, nutmeg, cloves, and salt. Beat in egg and flour. Add chopped almonds if using. Roll dough to 1/8-inch thickness on a lightly floured board and cut into shapes. Windmills and Sinterklaas/Santa shapes are traditional, or you can cut them into a child's initials. Decorate with whole almonds if using. Place one inch apart on lightly greased cookie sheets. Bake at 350°F for 8 to 10 minutes, or until the edges are lightly browned. Cool for one minute then transfer to wire racks to cool completely.

Oliebollen

A traditional Dutch doughnut.

Serves 4 to 6

Ingredients
2 cups milk
1 tablespoon sugar
1/2 teaspoon salt
2 tablespoons butter
1/4 cup warm water
1 small package cake yeast
1 egg
3 cups flour
1/2 cup raisins

Directions
Scald milk, stir in sugar, salt, and butter. Let cool. Pour warm water in a bowl and sprinkle in yeast. Stir until dissolved. Add milk mixture, egg, 1/2 cup of flour, and raisins. Beat until smooth. Stir in remaining flour. Cover and let rise for 1 hour or until it doubles in size. Beat batter down and deep fry spoonfuls of dough until brown. Sprinkle with powdered sugar when done.

Chocoladevla (Chocolate Pudding)

Serves 6

Ingredients
3 cups milk
3 tablespoons cornstarch
1 ounce cocoa
6 tablespoons sugar

Directions
Mix some milk with the cocoa and the cornstarch until there are no more lumps. Heat the remaining milk. Add the cocoa and cornstarch mixture and stir well until smooth, being sure to smooth out all the lumps. Let the mixture cook for about 3 minutes. Add the sugar to the pudding. Let cool.

After it has cooled, mix again with a hand mixer to eliminate all lumps. Pour into pudding bowls and refrigerate. Serve with fresh whipped cream.

Project and Report Ideas

Maps

- Make a map of the eurozone, and create a legend to indicate key manufacturing industries throughout the EU.
- Create an export map of the Netherlands using a legend to represent all the major products manufactured there. The map should clearly indicate all of the Netherlands' industrial regions.

Reports

- Write a brief report on Dutch agriculture.
- Write a report on Dutch concerns within the EU.
- Write a brief report on any of the following historical events: Dutch colonialism, World War I, World War II.

Biographies

Write a one-page biography on one of the following:

- Anne Frank
- Queen Beatrix
- Vincent van Gogh
- M. C. Escher

Journal

- Imagine you are a student in the Netherlands who is finishing primary school. Write a journal about the three different school options open to you. Each one has some advantages. You are not sure what to do. Finally you make a choice. Your journal should tell why you have chosen that option.
- Read more about the Dutch resistance movement during World War II. Imagine you are a student during the Nazi occupation. Write a journal about your life and what you can contribute to the resistance movement.

Projects

- Learn the Dutch expressions for simple words such as hello, good day, please, thank you. Try them on your friends.
- Make a calendar of your country's festivals and list the ones that are common or similar in the Netherlands. Do the Dutch celebrate them differently? If so, how?
- Go online or to the library and find images of The Hague's royal palaces. Create a model of one.
- Make a poster advertising Dutch tourism.
- Make a list of all the rivers, places, seas, and islands that you have read about in this book and indicate them on a map of the Netherlands.
- Find a Dutch recipe other than the ones given in this book, and ask an adult to help you make it. Share it with members of your class.
- Make a carnival mask that is a caricature of a leader in your community.
- Select a favorite Dutch artist and create a work of art in the same style.

Group Activities

- Debate: One side should take a position supporting the adoption of the European constitution and the other side against it.
- Debate: Discuss the custom of Sinterklaas and the traditional black face paint worn by his helpers. What are the implications of this tradition in a modern, multicultural society? Is it more important to preserve the traditions of the past or to accommodate the sensitivities of the society's newest members?

Chronology

4100 BCE	The Dolmen's erect prehistoric inhabitants of Dutch territory.
600 BCE	Germanic tribes occupy the area.
100 CE	Romans establish control over the region, which they name Germania Minor.
496	Franks gain control of Dutch territory and begin to convert the people to Christianity.
962	The Holy Roman Empire is established.
1548	Hapsburg ruler Charles V grants the "Pragmatic Sanction" granting the Netherlands a measure of autonomy.
1568	The Eighty Years' War begins.
1579	The Republic of the Seven United Netherlands is formed.
1602	The Dutch East India Company is incorporated.
1648	The Eighty Years' War ends, and the republic is granted independence.
1795	Napoleon invades the Netherlands.
1815	The Dutch monarchy is established.
1848	The Netherlands becomes a constitutional monarchy.
1914	World War I begins; the Netherlands remains neutral.
1922	Women are granted the right to vote.
1940	Nazi Germany invades the Netherlands.
1944	Operation Market-Garden liberates the southern portion of the country.
1945	The Allies liberate the rest of the country from the Nazis.
1945	The Netherlands becomes a charter member of the United Nations.
1949	The Netherlands becomes a founding member of NATO.
1957	The European Economic Community begins between Germany, France, Belgium, Italy, Luxembourg, and the Netherlands.
1992	The Maastricht Treaty is signed, creating the EU.
2002	The Netherlands adopts the euro.

FURTHER READING/INTERNET RESOURCES

Carlson, Linda. *UnDutchables: An Observation of the Netherlands, Its Culture and Its Inhabitants.* Lafayette, Colo.: White-Boucke Publishing, 2001.

Davis, Kevin. *Look What Came from the Netherlands.* New York: Scholastic Library Publishing, 2001.

De Roo, Gert. *Environmental Planning in the Netherlands: Too Good to Be True: From Command and Control Planning to Shared Governance.* Hampshire, UK: Ashgate Publishing, 2003.

Reynolds, Simon, Roseline Ngcheong-Lum, and Dorothy L. Gibbs. *Welcome to the Netherlands.* Milwaukee, Wis.: Gareth Stevens, 2002.

Van Zanden, Jan L. *The Economic History of the Netherlands 1914–1995: A Small Open Economy in the Long Twentieth Century.* Oxford, UK: Routledge, 1997.

Travel Information
www.lonelyplanet.com/destinations/europe/netherlands
www.virtualtourist.com/travel/ Europe/Netherlands/TravelGuide-Netherlands.html

History and Geography
www.infoplease.com
www.wikipedia.org

Culture and Festivals
www.nlembassy.org
www.powerofculture.nl

Economic and Political Information
www.cia.gov
www.wikipedia.org

EU Information
europa.eu.int/

FOR MORE INFORMATION

Netherlands Embassy
4200 Linnean Avenue NW
Washington, DC 20008
Tel.: 202-244-5300
Fax: 202-362-3430

Embassy of the United States in The Netherlands
Lange Voorhout 102
2514 EJ The Hague
The Netherlands
Tel.: 31-70-310-9209
Fax: 31-70-361-4688

Netherlands Ministry of Foreign Affairs
PO Box 20061, 2500 EB
The Hague, The Netherlands
Tel.: 31-70-348-6486
Fax.: 31-70-348-4848

European Union
Delegation of the European Commission to the United States
2300 M Street NW
Washington, DC 20037
Tel.: 202-862-9500
Fax: 202-429-1766

GLOSSARY

Allies: Nations united to fight the Axis powers during World War II.

aristocracy: People of noble families or the highest social class.

automated: Converted a process or work-place to one that replaces or minimizes human labor with mechanical or electronic machines or processes.

autonomous: Politically independent and self-governing.

autonomy: Political independence.

biomass: Plant and animal material used as a source of fuel.

blocs: United groups of countries.

Calvinism: The religious doctrine of John Calvin, which emphasizes that salvation comes through faith in God, and that God has already chosen those who will believe and be saved.

capital: Wealth in the form of money or property.

civil wars: Wars between opposing groups within a country.

cockade: A rosette, ribbon, or other orna-ment usually worn on a hat as an identifying badge.

concentration camps: Prison camps used for the extermination of prisoners under the rule of Adolf Hitler in Nazi Germany.

constitutional monarchy: A political sys-tem in which the head of state is a king or queen ruling to the extent allowed by a constitu-tion.

deforestation: removal of trees from an area of land.

delta: A triangular deposit of sand and soil at the mouth of a river or inlet.

democratic: Characterized by free and equal participation in government or a decision-making process of an organization or group.

deportation: The forcible expulsion of a for-eign national from a country.

dikes: Embankments built along the shore of a sea or lake or beside a river to hold back the water and prevent flooding.

duchies: Territories over which a duke or duchess rules.

entrepreneurial: Characteristic of one who assumes the risks and responsibilities of running a business.

euthanasia: The practice of killing or allow-ing the death of hopelessly sick individuals.

excise: A government-imposed tax on domestic goods.

extortion: The crime of obtaining something, such as money, from somebody using illegal methods of persuasion.

feudal: Relating to feudalism, the legal and social system that existed in medieval Europe in which vassals held land from lords in exchange for military service.

Great Depression: The drastic decline in the world economy resulting in mass unemployment and widespread poverty that lasted from 1929 until 1939.

greenhouse effect: The warming of the earth's surface as a result of atmospheric pollution by gasses.

gross domestic product (GDP): The total value of all goods and services produced in a country in a year, minus the net income from investments in other countries.

homogeneous: Having a uniform structure.

hunter-gatherers: Members of a society in which people live by hunting and gathering only, with no livestock or crops raised for food.

hydraulic engineering: Engineering involving the science that deals with practical applications of liquid in motion.

ice age: Any of the periods in earth's history when temperatures fell worldwide and large areas of the surface was covered with glaciers.

infrastructure: A country's large-scale public systems, services, and facilities that are necessary for economic activity.

integration: The process of opening a group, community, place, or organization to all.

liberal: Tolerant of different views and standards of behavior.

lynched: Hanged without trial.

miniaturization: The act of making a version of something in a much smaller size or on a greatly reduced scale.

nationalist: Someone who is proudly loyal and devoted to a nation.

neutral: Not favoring sides in a conflict.

Paleolithic: The early part of the Stone Age.

pragmatic: Practical.

precursor: Something that comes before something else, and is often considered to have lead to the development of another thing.

principalities: Territories ruled by a prince or princess.

quota: A proportional share of something.

ratified: Officially approved.

rationing: Distributing something in fixed quantities.

recession: A decline in economic trade and activity lasting for a shorter length of time than a depression.

referendum: A vote by the whole of an electorate on a specific question or questions put to it by a government or similar body.

secession: A formal withdrawal from an organization, state, or alliance.

secular: Not controlled by a religious authority or concerned with spiritual or religious matters.

service sector: The segment of business that sells services rather than products.

sluices: Artificial channels for the flow of water.

solidarity: Unity.

sovereignty: Freedom from external control.

stagnancy: A period of inactivity.

sustainable: Capable of being maintained.

tariff: A government-imposed tax on imports.

temperate maritime: A climate characterized by a lack of extremes and influenced by the sea.

tributaries: Streams feeding a larger stream or river.

tundra: A level treeless plain characteristic of arctic or subarctic regions and consisting of black mucky soil with a permanently frozen subsoil.

vested: Having a stake in something.

INDEX

Picture Credits

Corel: pp. 16–17, 24, 27, 28, 30–31, 34, 37, 38–39, 40, 43, 46–47, 49, 66–67, 70, 72

Used with permission of the European Communities: pp. 52–53, 55, 58, 61, 62

Photos.com: pp: 10–11, 13, 14, 19, 20, 23, 33, 44, 50, 56, 65, 69

BIOGRAPHIES

AUTHOR

Heather Docalavich first developed an interest in the history and cultures of Eastern Europe through her work as a genealogy researcher. She currently resides in Hilton Head, South Carolina, with her four children.

SERIES CONSULTANTS

Ambassador John Bruton served as Irish Prime Minister from 1994 until 1997. As prime minister, he helped turn Ireland's economy into one of the fastest-growing in the world. He was also involved in the Northern Ireland Peace Process, which led to the 1998 Good Friday Agreement. During his tenure as Ireland's prime minister, he also presided over the European Union presidency in 1996 and helped finalize the Stability and Growth Pact, which governs management of the euro. Before being named the European Commission Head of Delegation in the United States, he was a member of the convention that drafted the European Constitution, signed October 29, 2004.

The European Commission Delegation to the United States represents the interests of the European Union as a whole, much as ambassadors represent their countries' interests to the U.S. government. Matters coming under European Commission authority are negotiated between the commission and the U.S. administration.